WordPress:

How to Build your Own Website with WordPress for Beginners

Table of Contents

Introduction

Websites are now a common way of providing information to people and getting services online. You may need to develop a website for your business or even a personal blog. WordPress is a good platform that can help you do this with much easy. Web development is known to be a complex task that involves writing thousands of computer programming line codes. With WordPress, you can develop a website without writing even a single line of code. This book guides you on how to do this. Enjoy reading!

Chapter 1- Getting Started with WordPress

WordPress is a content management system (CMS) used for development of dynamic websites and blogs. WordPress forms the most popular blogging system that is available on the web today. It enables its users to use its back end to update and customize their website. WordPress is an open source CMS.

WordPress was first introduced in 2003 as a way of adding content to a website without having to write even a single line of code. With WordPress, you don't have to know computer programming in order to develop a website. Since then, WordPress has grown exponentially and it is now used by millions of websites that are seen by millions of people each day. It enables you to add widgets, themes and plugins to it, making it possible for you to develop any type of website that you need.

Although it is true that you can develop a website with WordPress without having to write a single line of code, WordPress allows you to integrate your own PHP code if you need. You can use CSS to modify the theme for your WordPress site.

Installing WordPress

You can install WordPress on your computer (localhost) and develop your website from there. The following are the system requirements for you to be able to install WordPress:

1. Database. Use MySQL 5.0 +

2. Web Server. Use WAMP (Windows), LAMP (Linux), XAMP (Multi-platform), MAMP (Macintosh)

3. Operating System. WordPress is Cross-platform.

4. Browser. Use either IE (Internet Explorer 8+), Google chrome, Firefox, Safari or Opera

5. PHP 5.2+

Next, download WordPress from

https://wordpress.org/download/

You only have to click the "Download WordPress ..." button located to the right of the screen.

WordPress requires a MySQL database in your system. Login to your MySQL database as the root user then create an empty database that will be used by WordPress. You create an empty database and WordPress will create the necessary tables automatically in that database. During the installation, WordPress will ask you to specify the name of the database.

Now that you have created the database, it is time for you to setup the WordPress. Extract the WordPress package (setup) that you have downloaded then transfer it to web server or the localhost. If you are transferring it to the localhost and you are using WampServer, this is normally the "www" folder.

Next, open your browser then navigate to the path in which you have stored the WordPress. In my case, I have placed the WordPress in the www folder of WampServer installation. If I navigate to that directory on the browser, I am able to see it under the "Your Projects" tab:

Tools	Your Projects	Your Aliases	Your VirtualHost
phpinfo()	Easydrive	adminer	localhost
phpmyadmin	wordpress	phpmyadmin	
Add a Virtual Host		phpsysinfo	

Just click it. You will be asked to choose the language you need to use then click "Continue". In the next step, information about the database requirements will be shown. Read through then click ""Let's go".

In the next screen, enter information the MySQL database. The "Database Name" is the name of the MySQL database that you have created for the WordPress site. The "Username" is the name you use to log into the MySQL database. The Password is the password that you have created for MySQL database. The "Database Host" is the name of the host or computer, which takes a default value of "localhost". The "Table Prefix" value will be used as the prefix when giving names to the database tables.

Once you have completed filling all the information, click the "Submit" button. WordPress will check whether you have provided correct database information and you will get a confirmations screen. Click the button written "Run the install".

Next, you should provide the administrative information. The site title is the name of the website that you are developing. Also, enter a username and a password that you will be using to log into the administrative panel of the website. Also, ensure that you add your email address.

Once you have filled all the information that is required, click the "Install WordPress" button.

After a successful installation of WordPress, you will see a success screen. Click the "Log In" button then use the username and password that you created to login. After a successful login, you will be taken to the WordPress dashboard.

General Settings

It will be good for you to know more about the general WordPress before starting to develop your website. To access the general settings, move the mouse cursor to the bottom left of the screen. Click "Settings", and then choose "General".

The general settings page will then be displayed. It is possible for you change any details about the website from this change. Just fill all the details and once done, click the "Save Changes" button.

Chapter 2- Creating Pages

Pages are used for creation of static content. However, it is possible for you to modify or update a page anytime that you need. To see all the pages that you website currently has, move to the navigation bar on the left, click "Pages" then choose "All Pages".

You should note that a page is different from a post. Posts are simply blog entries that you enter from time to time. They are normally listed in a reverse chronological order. The pages can be related to the Home, About Us and Contact Us sections of your website.

For you to add a new page, click "Pages" then choose "Add New". Note that when creating a new page, you are not given an option to use tags or categories. It is possible for you to implement the parent-child relationship when creating pages. If you need to have a page that is a child of another page, you only have to indent the page column in menu section. It will then appear in the form of a drop down menu item from the parent page.

Note that a new page will not be added to the menu automatically. For you to do this, you should visit the Menu section then add the new page to custom menu.
You can find the Menu under Appearance in navigation section of the Dashboard. To add the page to menu, check the box on it then click "Add to Menu".

Editing Pages

WordPress allows you to edit the pages that you have created. The following steps will help you do this:

1. Click Pages then choose "All Pages".

2. Identify the page that you need to edit. However the mouse cursor over the pages and you will a number of

options displayed below the page that you need to edit. You can edit the page by clicking either "Edit" or "Quick Edit".

3. Click the "Edit" option. A new window will be shown. You will be allowed to change the title of the page as well as its contents in the way you need. After a successful update, click the "Update" button to save the changes.

4. You can also edit the page by clicking the "Quick Edit" option. Here, you will only be allowed to edit the title, the slug and date when the page was created. It is also possible for you to choose the parent for the page.

5. Once done with the update, click the "Update" button.

Chapter 3- Installing WordPress Themes

A WordPress theme allows you to control how your WordPress website looks like in terms of color, fonts, page layout etc. It is possible for you to get a free theme or pay and get a premium one. There are various websites that provide free as well as premium themes.

To manage your WordPress themes, click Appearance from the left navigation bar, then choose "Themes". For you to add a new Theme, you only have to click the "Add New" button. This will take you to a directory where you can get free themes. This is the wordpress.org website. Use filters or search in order to get the theme that you want. Choose theme that you need then click the "Preview" button in order to see how it looks like. If you like how it looks like, click the "Install" button.

You can choose a theme to use from your local drive. You should have downloaded the theme and saved it on your local computer. This is very helpful when you need to install a theme that is not listed in the Wordpress.org website. The theme can be uploaded from **Themes -> Install Themes** section. Click the "Upload Theme" button located at the top of the page.
Next, click "Browse" button, choose the archive of the theme you're your computer then click the "Install Now" button.

After some seconds, the theme will be uploaded then extracted for you. You will get a success message. To active the theme, just click "Activate" which will be shown as an option at the bottom of the success message.

However, the previous method is very simple. It even becomes simpler if you know the name of the theme that you need to use. It is always good for you to apply filters when searching for a theme. For example, if you need a theme with two columns, you must check the button for "Two Columns" when searching for a theme. Once you have checked all the filters that you need to use for search, click the "Apply Filters" button.

You will then be presented with all the themes that match your search criteria. You can then choose to install one of the themes. After a successful installation, you should activate the theme by clicking the "Activate" button. After that, go to the

Customizing WordPress Theme

You can use a theme customization tool in order to further customize the theme that you have chosen. You only have to click "Appearance" from the left menu, and then click "Customize". You will then be able to customize the current theme according to your needs by changing the colors, site identity, menus, background image, widgets and others.

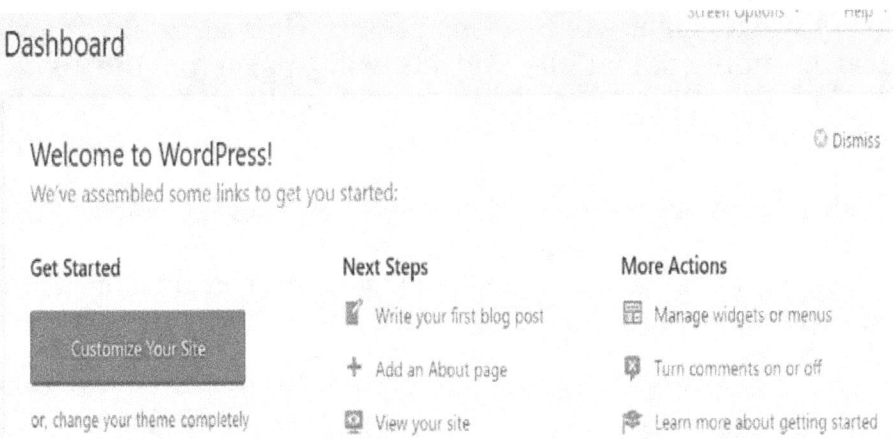

After clicking the "Customize" option, you will see a new screen. On the left side of the screen, you will have the customizing section, while the theme you have chosen to work with will be on the right side. In the section for "Active theme", you can click "Change" in order to change the theme which you are currently using. After clicking on "Change", you will be presented with a list of themes.

Choose the one you need to change to then click "Save & Continue". The new theme will be saved. In the section for "Site Title & Tagline", you will be able to add a title for the site as well as the tagline that you will want to add to the site.

It is also possible for you to change the color of your header text from the section for "Colors". As you scroll through the colors, you will observe that the right side of the page will keep on changing. You can also add your own color to the box between 'Current color' and 'Default'.

You can also add a header image from the "Header Image" section. You can choose from the suggestion or click "Add new image".

To add widgets to the site, click the > button to the right of "Widgets". You will see a window with two sections, that is, Main Widget Area and Secondary Widget Area. If you click in the section for Main Widget Area, you will be presented with a list of widgets that will be displayed at footer section. You will also be notified that the widgets will appear on the footer section of the site. After clicking on any of the widgets, you will see a dropdown from which you will be able to edit or even add more.

Example, if you are in need of adding categories, you will see an image with a title section and a number of checkboxes. The category can be added in the "Title" section. You can check any box that you need. If you don't need any of the boxes, just click "Remove.

For the case of Secondary Widget, you should click "Add a widget" and you will be provided with a sidebar that has a list of widgets. Click the one you need and it will be added to your widget list.

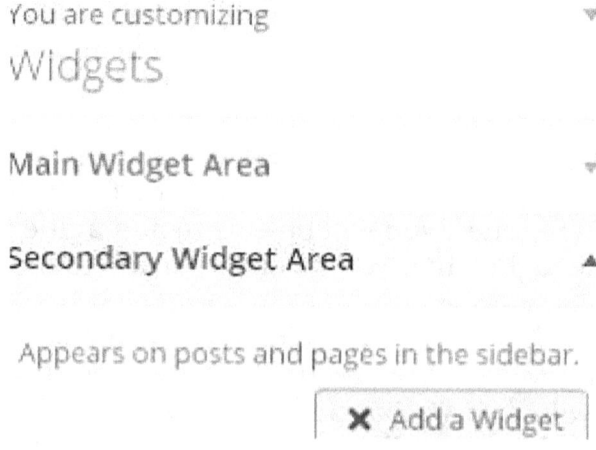

By clicking the "Add a Widget" button, you will be able to add as many widgets as you need. For the case of the front page, you can choose to display either a static page or your latest posts.

That is it. That is how you can use WordPress to change the look of your website.

Chapter 4- Installing WordPress Plugins

Plugins provide you with an easy way to customize modify and enhance a WordPress blog or post. The plugin is simply software that you can upload in order to expand the functionality of your site. Plugins are used to add features to a WordPress website or blog. Plugins exist for almost everything. You can use plugins to share your website content on social media. You can also use plugins for web security purpose, as well as get information on how people have been visiting your website. Plugins can also be used for search engine optimization.

To see all the plugins that have been currently installed on your WordPress website, click on "Plugins" from the left navigation bar then click "Installed Plugins". You will see a new window which has a column for plugin name and the description for the plugin. For you to add a new plugin, you should add its files to the wp-content/plugins directory. After an installation of the plugin, you can activate or deactivate it from the Plugins menu.

If you need to install a particular plugin to your website, begin by downloading it to your computer. Next, on the administration panel of WordPress, navigate to the left navigation bar then click Plugins.
 Choose "Add New". Browse to where you have stored the plugin in your computer then select it. Next, click "Install Now" and you will have the plugin installed. You can also find the plugin that you want by choosing from the Featured, Popular, Recommended **and** Favorites sections, or even by typing the name of the plugin in the search field in order to search for it.

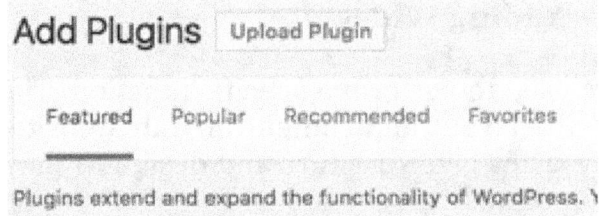

After a complete installation of the plugin, you must activate it by pressing the "Activate" button.

The removal of a plugin can also be done with much ease. You only have to remove the directory which has the plugin that you need to uninstall and it will be deactivated automatically. Also, it is worth noting that the process of installation of different plugins is not the same. It will always good for you to refer to its documentation as well as the installation instructions.

Also, when downloading a WordPress plugin, it is good for one to check whether it is compatible with the version of WordPress that you are using.
Ensure that you check for the date when the plugin was lastly updated. It will also be good for you to check for the ratings that your plugin has. If you use an outdated or a poor quality plugin, you may have problems with your website.

Chapter 5- Adding Widgets

Widgets are used to perform a specific function. They can help you change the layout and content of your website easily and very quickly. They give structure and design to the WordPress theme that one is using.

You can access the Widgets section from the dashboard by clicking the "Appearance" from the left navigation bar. You will be presented with a list of the available widgets. There are areas on the sides on which you are allowed to place widgets. By default, one should have sections for Primary Sidebar, Content Sidebar, and Footer Widget Area. Note that the number of the available widgets will be determined by the WordPress theme that you are using.

For you to add a widget, expand the area in which you need to have the widget, drag then drop the widget there then click "Save". Whenever you need to remove a widget, you only have to drag it out of the widget area. If you are in need of adding your own text to the widget, select a plain text widget then add your HTML or text on it.

Chapter 6- WordPress Posts

In WordPress, it is easy for you to add new content by creating a new post. The posts are sometimes known as blog posts or articles. They are normally used to make one's blog popular.

Adding a New Post

The following steps will help you add a new post to your website:

1. Move the mouse cursor to the navigation pane on the left then click on "Posts". Choose "Add New".

2. The editor page will be presented to you. The WordPress WYSIWYG editor can help you create the content for the post.

   You will notice that the window has two tabs, the Visual and Text tabs. The visual tab will show you how the content will appear when published on the website. The text tab shows you the content of the post in HTML format. The post editor toolbar has a number of tools that will help you format the content of your post. Example, you can write the text in bold, italics etc. You can also add media such as photos and videos to the post.

   The Draft button on the right hand side will help you save your post in the form of a draft then come to it later. The Preview button next to the Draft button will help you see how the post will appear once published to the website.

You are also provided with an option that will help you change the visibility of the post. If you choose the Public option, the post will stick to the front page. You can also schedule the post to be published later rather than publishing it immediately.

Down this, there is a part where you can choose the Category for the post as well as add tags to it.

In the field for "Post Title", enter the title of the post. In the field for "Post Content", enter the post content.

3. You can then publish the post by clicking the "Publish" button located on the right side.

Anytime that you need to delete the post, just click "Move to Trash" and it will be deleted.

Editing Posts

After publishing your post, you may need to edit it. The following steps will help you do this:

1. Click "Posts" then choose "All Posts".

2. Identify the post that you need to edit. However the mouse cursor over the post and you will get a number of options. There are two ways through which you can edit the post, that is, Edit and Quick Edit. Click Edit below the title of the post then change the title or the content of the post as you need. To save the changes, click the Update button. The post will be changed and the changes will be updated.

   The Quick Edit option will allow you to change the Title, the Date and Slug of the post. You can also choose the category for the post then you click "Update".

Deleting Posts

The following steps will help you delete the WordPress posts that you don't need:

1. Click Posts, and then choose "All Posts".

2. However the mouse cursor over the post that you need to delete and you will see a number of options displayed below it. Click "Trash" and the post will be deleted.

3. You can then view the list of all posts to see whether the post has been deleted.

Previewing a Post

It will be good for you to preview a post before you can publish it. This will help you know how the post will look like on the website so that you can make any necessary corrections before making it available to the users. The followi9ng steps will help you do this:

1. Click on Posts then choose "All Posts".

2. However the mouse cursor over the post name and see the options that are displayed. Click on the "View" option.

Other than the above steps, you can click the "Preview" option while editing or adding the post and you will be shown how it will appear on your website.

Chapter 7- Categories

When adding posts to your website, it is good to make it easy to find a particular post. With categories, you are able to group your posts into various subjects in order to make them easy to find. This means that with categories, you are able to group the posts that are related. The following steps will help you create a new category for your posts:

1. Click on Posts, and then choose Categories.

2. You will see the categories page displayed for you. The following fields should be filled:

   Name- This is the name for the category. Each category should have a unique name.

   Slug- this is a name that you use to describe the post. You should specify it in the tags URL.

   Parent- if you choose the parent category from the dropdown, you will be able to set the particular category as a sub-category or just keep it as none.

   Description- This is where you should add a description for your category. This is optional.

3. Once you have filled all the information needed for the category, click the "Add New Category" button. The new category that you have just created will be shown on the right side of the page.

Editing a Category

Sometimes, you may need to edit the categories that you have. This can be done by following the steps given below:

1. Click on Posts then choose Categories.

2. However the mouse cursor over the categories. A number of options will be displayed under category name. You can choose either "Edit" or "Quick Edit" in order to edit the category. Click the "Edit" option in order to edit any of the fields that will be presented to you. Once done, click "Update" for the changes to be saved. You will notice that the presented fields are similar to the ones presented while you were creating the category.

3. You can also click the "Quick Edit" option. You will only be allowed to edit the title and the slug of the category. Once done with editing, click the "Update Category" button.

Arranging Categories

It is possible for you to change the arrangement of categories in WordPress. However, for you to be able to arrange the categories the way you want, you must download then install the Category Order plugin. After the installation of the plugin, follow the steps given below:

1. Click "Posts" then choose "Category Order". The option for "Category Order" will be added once you have installed the Category Order plugin.

2. A screen will be presented to you, and you will be able to see that the categories are not in order. To reorder them, you only have to drag them and arrange them the way you need. Once you done with dragging them, click the "Order Categories" button in order to save the changes.

Deleting Categories

Sometimes, you may need to delete one of the categories that you have. The following steps can help you do this:

1. Click Posts, and then choose Categories.

2. However the mouse cursor over the categories and you will see a number of options displayed. Click the "Delete" option in order to delete the option.

3. You will get a pop up with a message asking you to confirm the deletion of the category. Click the "OK" button of the popup in order to confirm the deletion.

Chapter 8- Tags

Unlike categories, tags are used to create a number of groups that fit into various categories. A good example of a category is beauty, while hair, eyes, and lips form the tags.

You can see a tag as small information that is attached to the main content or a post in order to identify it. If you mention the tag in the correct way, then it will be easy for you to find the post or the content.

The following steps will help you add tags:

1. Click on "Posts" then choose "Tags". The tags page will be presented to you.

2. You will be required to provide the tag name, slug and description.

```
Add New Tag

Name

|

The name is how it appears on your site.


Slug


The "slug" is the URL-friendly version of the
name. It is usually all lowercase and contains
only letters, numbers, and hyphens.


Description




The description is not prominent by default;
however, some themes may show it.

Add New Tag
```

3. The name should be the name for the tags. The slug is simply a word that you choose to be used as a description for your post. It should be defined in tags URL. You should also give a brief description of your tag. The description will be shown any time that you however the mouse cursor over it.

4. Once you provided all the required information, scroll to the bottom then click the "Add New Tag" button.

5. You will see the new tags that you have just created displayed on the right side of the window.

Editing Tags

Once you have created tags in WordPress, it is possible for you to edit them. To edit your tags, follow the steps given below:

Click Posts then choose Tags.

Identify the tag that you need to edit. However the mouse cursor over the tags and you will see a number of options displayed. You can click either "Edit" or Quick Edit" in order to edit the tag.

Click Edit. Edit any of the fields that are presented to you and once done, click the "Update" button to save the changes. Note that this option presents you with fields that you saw when adding the tag.

You can also edit the tag by clicking the "Quick Edit" option. Here, you will only be required to edit the name and the slug for the tag. Once done with the editing, click the "Update Tag" button and the changes will be saved.

Deleting Tags

If you need to delete tags, follow the steps given below:

1. Click on Posts, and then choose Tags.

2. However the mouse cursor over the tags and you will see a number of options displayed. Click the Delete option which will help you delete the tag.

3. After clicking the Delete option, you will be presented with a pop up that asks you to confirm the deletion of the tag. Just click the OK button to confirm the deletion. The tag will then be deleted permanently.

Chapter 9- Adding Media

WordPress has a Media library which is made up of images, videos and audios that you can upload and add it to your content anytime that you are creating a new post or a page. You will also be allowed to delete any media files that you don't need.

The following steps will help you know how to use the WordPress Media library:

1. On the navigation bar on the left side of the screen, click "Media" then choose "Library".

2. All the media files such as images, audios and videos will be shown on the page. Click the "Add New" button.

3. You will be presented with a new window for "Upload New Media". You can and drop the media files into the provided window, or just click the "Select Files" option. You will be seeing the files dialog open up, and you will be able to browse throughout the computer for the files.

You will also be provided with buttons which you can click and have different views of the media files.
For example, you can click the List View button and view the files in a list form. The Grid View button will help you view the images in a grid form. You are provided with a search box where you can search for an image by writing its name there.

Adding New Media

WordPress accepts media files in the form of audio, video or image. These can be added as follows:

1. Click Media then choose "Add New".

2. You will be taken to a new window. On the window, click the "Select Files" option displayed at the center.

A files dialog will appear that will allow you to browse to where you have kept the files on your computer.

3. Navigate to where you have stored them then choose files such as videos, audios and images. Once done, click the "Open" button. The media files will then be loaded to WordPress.

Inserting Media

Now that you have uploaded your media files into the libraries, it is time for you to insert them into your posts and pages. The following are the steps necessary for you to insert media in WordPress:

1. Click Media, and then choose "Add New".

2. Click "Add Media".

3. Click "Media Library" tab so as to insert the media files from the media library. These should be the files that you had uploaded previously.

On the right side of your screen, you will see information regarding the media file that you have selected below "Attachment Details". Click the "Insert Media" button and the media will be inserted into the post. In the section for "Attachment Details", you will be able to see regarding the media files such as the Title, URL, Caption, Description and Alt Text.

It is also possible for you to insert images directly from your computer. This can be done from the "Upload Files" tab. Once done with the upload, click the "Insert into Post" button.

Editing Media

Even after adding media to the media library, it is possible for you to edit it from there. The following steps will help you edit your media saved in WordPress:

1. Click Media then choose Library. Click the name of the item you need to edit or click the edit link.

2. You will be presented with the list of the available media files. Select the one you need to edit.

3. The page for editing the media will have a number of options on the right side.

4. Edit all the fields that you need to edit then click the "Update" button in order to save the changes.

Chapter 10- Backing Up a WordPress Website

Creating a backup of a WordPress is a way of ensuring that your entire website is kept in an alternative location for safety purposes. If something wrong happens with your WordPress website, it will be possible for you to recover all the files to their original condition.

It is recommended that you frequently take a backup of your site so that you don't fall into trouble. This will make it easy for you to get back to your original condition after you have a made a change to the website or deleted an important element.

Using WordPress Plugin

The All-In-One WP Migration plugin can help you to create a backup of your WordPress site. Install via the steps we discussed in the chapter for installing plugins. It will provide you with options for Import, Export and Backup. Click on "Export" in order to open the Export Site screen then choose the "Export To" button. You will then be asked to choose the place where you need to save the files from the exported WordPress website. The following options will be provided:

- File
- FTP
- DropBox
- Google Drive
- Amazon S3
- OneDrive
- Box

EXPORT SITE   REPORT ISSUE

Find <text> Replace with <another-text> in the database   >

ADD

> Advanced options (click to expand)

EXPORT TO   —

FILE

FTP

DROPBOX

GOOGLE DRIVE

AMAZON S3

ONEDRIVE

BOX

If you need to save the exported website just on your computer, just choose the first choice. Next, click the "Download" option and you will be done.

After that, you will be in a position to Import all the safeguarded website files and the database onto the new or existing WordPress instance by following almost similar steps. The difference should be, after installing the All-In-One WP Migration plugin onto the new website, just choose the Import option rather than the Export option. After a successful import, you will be in a position to see all your images, themes, videos and other details of your website as they were at the time the backup was created.

Using FTP

Other than the use of a plugin, there are several other ways of creating a backup for a WordPress site. You can use a FTP (File Transfer Protocol) client such as Filezilla or Cyberduck to create easily create a backup of your WordPress site. This is the best method for you to create the backup if you are unable to access the admin part of the website.

The following steps will help you create a backup of your WordPress website using FTP. Ensure that you have installed the Filezilla on your system:

1. Begin by opening the Filezilla client.

2. Enter the necessary details for you to login to the cPanel. The details include the Host, Username, Password and the Port that are needed for you to establish a connection.

3. Once you have filled all the necessary details, click the "QuickConnect" button.

4. All the files and folders of your WordPress site will be shown on the right side of the screen.

5. Select all the files and folders. Right click your mouse cursor then choose "Download".

Once the files and folders for the website have been downloaded, they will be saved on your system.

Database Backup

Now that you have backed up the files for the site, you can go ahead and backup the WordPress database. The following steps will help do this:

1. Begin by opening the browser then type the following URL:

http://localhost/phpmyadmin

2. The home page for phpMyAdmin will be opened. This should appear as shown below:

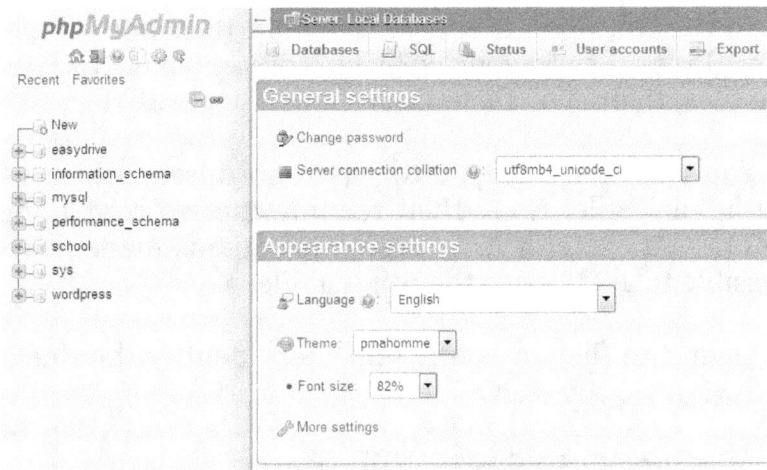

On the left side of the screen will be a list of database that you have created in MySQL. Identify the name of the database that you created for your WordPress website then click it.

3. The database will be opened and you will see the list of the tables that it has. On the top bar of the new screen, click the "Export" option.

4. You will be provided with two ways through which you can export your database, that is, Quick and Custom. Choose any of the methods then click the "Go" button.

Once the database file is exported, it will be saved on your local system.

Restoring the WordPress Files

You can use FTP to restore the files for your WordPress site. The following steps will help you achieve this:

1. Begin by launching the Filezilla client then login to the cPanel using the necessary credentials.

2. In the ftp, open the local directory then upload all your WordPress files to your website. You only have to select all the files, right click them then choose "Upload".

3. You can then navigate to "your wordpress folder -> wp-config.php" file. Copy then rename the wp-config.php file before you can edit it. In case a mistake is made, it will be possible to get back to the original file.

4. Open the file wp-config.php then identify the line given below:

define('DB_NAME', 'db_name');

Replace the db_name with the name of the database that you created.

define('DB_USER', 'db_user');
Replace the db_user with your MySQL username.

define('DB_PASSWORD', 'db_password');

Replace the db_password with the password for the above MySQL user.

Once you have made all the above changes to the file, save it then use ftp to upload it to your website.

Restoring the WordPress Database

The following steps will help you restore your WordPress database:

1. Open the phpMyAdmin by typing the following URL on your browser:

http://localhost/phpmyadmin

You can choose to create a new database or import from the backup you had created earlier. Just create a new database by clicking the "Databases" tab. Type the name of the database, example, "mysite" then click the "Create" button.

The new database name will be added to the list of the names of the available databases. Just click the database name.

2. Next, click the "Import" option on the toolbar located at the top. You can then click the "Choose File" option in order to find the backup file from the system. Once you have uploaded the backup SQL file, choose the format as sql.

3. You can then click the "Go" button.

4. Once the upload of the file is done successfully, you will get a message notifying you that it was successful.

Chapter 11- Spam Protection

It is good for you to protect your website from spam. WordPress comes preinstalled with Akismet, which is an antispam solution. This is why you should keep your WordPress script updated.

It is possible for you to activate Akismet, but you must have the WordPress API Key. You must register yourself at the official WordPress website. They will then send the key to your mail box. To activate the protection of your website from spam using Akismet Spam Protection plugin, follow the steps given below:

1. Open the dashboard of your WordPress website. Click on "Plugins" then choose "Installed".

2. Akismet will be in the list of the installed plugins. Click the "Activate" button which is located just below it. This will activate the Akismet plugin.

3. Next, click the option for "Activate your Akismet Account".

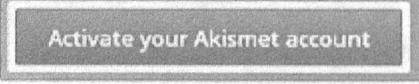

4. In the next window, move the mouse cursor to the right of the screen, then click the "Get your API key" button. This will give you a new API key. If you already have the key, you can enter it manually.

5. In case you don't have the API key, just click the "GET AN AKISMET API KEY" tab so that you can move further. You will be asked to provide values for the following fields:

Signing up for **Akismet** with WordPress.com

I already have a WordPress.com account!

E-mail Address

Username

Password

Fill the fields then click the "Sign Up" button located at the bottom of the screen.

1. After completing the registration process, the API key will be send to the inbox of your registered email address. Type the API Key manually then once done, click the "Use this key" button.

2. If the API key that you enter is correct, it will be verified successfully and you will get a confirmation message on the screen.

3. After the above steps, your website will be protected against spams by Akismet. If it is a blog and you have the comments section, you will be able to check the comments left by users for spam. You will also be able to automatically mark some comments as spam from the Comments section of the admin area.

It will be possible for you to track the number of spam posts that have been stopped by the Akismet and be able to secure your comments, posts etc. It will also be possible for you to protect your website from spammers who are capable of harming your website.

Chapter 12- Links

Once you have created WordPress pages, you can add links to them. A link helps you connect one source to another. This means that after adding links to your website pages, you will be able to connect to pages from other websites or even the same website.

The following steps will help you add links in WordPress:

1. Click "Pages", and then choose "All Pages".

2. A new screen will be showing all the pages that you have created on WordPress. Identify the page that you need to add link(s) to then select it by a click.

3. You had added content to the website in the form of a text. Identify the text that you need to add a link to then highlight it.

4. The editor's bar has several tools, including the "Insert/Edit Link" icon. Click this icon and you will see the following window:

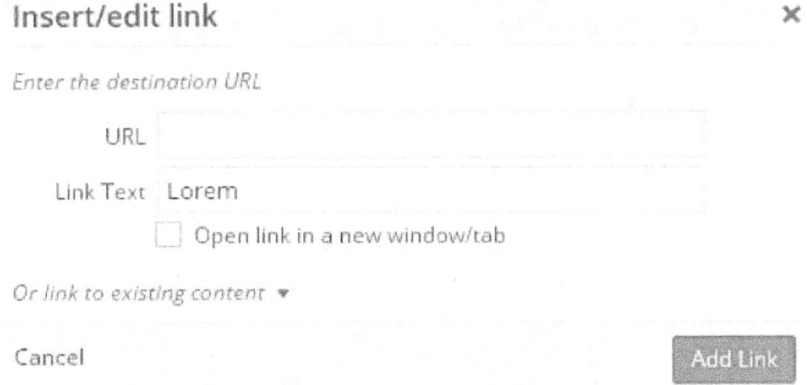

5. You will be able to see the following fields:

   • URL- here enters the URL that you need to link.

- Link text- here; add the text that you need to enter into your link.

- Open link in a new window/tab- if you check this checkbox, the page for the link will be opened in a new tab/window once the user clicks the link.

- Or link to existing account- this allows you to link to an existing page, that is, a page that you have created. You only have to select the page from the drop down. If you click the drop down, the list of the available pages will be displayed, so your work will only be to select the page that you need to link to. Posts that you have created will also be part of the list. Once you have selected the post or page that you need to link to, the links will be created in the URL field. You can then click "Add Link".

6. You can However on the text that you chose to create the link for. The link will be displayed.

7. Now that everything is okay, click the "Update" to save the changes to your page or post.

How to Edit a Link

Once you have created a link in WordPress, it is possible for you to edit it. The following steps can help you do this:

1. Click on "Pages", and then select "All Pages".

2. The list of the available pages will be shown. Identify the page that has the link that you need to edit. However the mouse cursor on the name of the page and you will get a number of options. Click the "Edit" option.

3. You will see the text for which you had created a link. However the mouse cursor on this text. You will see a pencil symbol. Click the symbol in order to edit the link.

4. You can simply edit the link or change it by selecting the page you need to link to from the list. Select the page or the post from your list, click the "Update" button.

5. However the mouse cursor on the text you chose to add a link to and see whether the correct link is shown in the form of a tooltip text.

6. You can then click the "Update" button in order to save the changes that you have made to your page or post.

How to Delete a Link

Sometimes, your web page or articles may have links that you don't want to use any longer. This calls for you to delete the link. The following steps will help you delete a link from your WordPress page or post:

1. Click on "Pages" then choose "All Pages".

2. You will be presented with a page that has all the pages that you have created. However the mouse cursor on the page with the link that you need to delete and you will see a number of options displayed.

3. Click the "Edit" option.

4. Select the word for which you had created a link. The editor's toolbar located at the top has an icon for "Remove Link" symbol. This is shown below:

Click the icon in order to remove the link.

5. Verify whether the link has been deleted by However the mouse cursor on the text you had the link for. If you don't see the tooltip, this is an indication that the link has been deleted. If you see the tooltip, the link has not been deleted, so you must repeat all the above steps.

6. Lastly, click the "Update" button to save the changes that you have made to the site.

Chapter 13- Transferring WordPress

Sometimes, you may need to transfer your WordPress website to a new hosting platform. This is possible. The transfer can be done from Wordpress.com or from any other hosting platform.

The task of migrating the WordPress site from one hosting platform to another platform consists of the following three major steps:

1. Move the files.

2. Move the WordPress database.

3. Do the reconfiguration.

Move the Files

You can use the FTP client that you need when moving WordPress files from one host to another. If the old host uses a cPanel, create a .zip archive for the website file using a File Manager tool. You can then transfer the zipped files to the new host then you unzip them. This will help you save much of your time since transferring one large file is faster compared to transferring many small files.

Move the WordPress Database

Now that you have moved the files for your WordPress site, you should move the database. You should begin by exporting the database from your old account. We discussed this in one of our previous chapters. Once the database export is done, create a database in your new host then import the exported data into it. This was also discussed previously.

Reconfiguration

After the above, you should reconfigure your WordPress so that it can use the values of the new database. To do this, navigate to the root folder of WordPress then open the wp-config.php file. Find the following lines from the file:

define('DB_NAME', 'db');
/ MySQL database username */**
define('DB_USER', 'username');
/ MySQL database password */**
define('DB_PASSWORD', 'password');
/ MySQL hostname */**
define('DB_HOST', 'hostname');

You must set the correct values for the parameters given above.
The "db" should be replaced with the database name, the "username" with the name of the database user, the "password" with the corresponding user password and the "hostname" with the new host in which you have transferred the WordPress.

After that you will be done and ready to use WordPress in your new setup!

Conclusion

This marks the end of this book. WordPress is a content management system that you can use to create a website or a blog. When creating a blog or a website with WordPress, you don't have to write even a single line of code. This makes it the best option for individuals who don't have knowledge in computer programming. Creating a website with WordPress also takes you the shortest time possible. This makes it the best option when you need to have a website urgently. To enhance the look and feel of your WordPress website, choose and use the best themes.

There are several WordPress themes that you can download and use for free but there are others for which you have to pay in order to download and use them. Widgets and Plugins are also good in WordPress as they help you extend the functionality of the platform by providing you with additional features. With WordPress, you can also transfer your website from one host to another and it will work with no difference.

www.ingramcontent.com/pod-product-compliance
Lightning Source LLC
Chambersburg PA
CBHW071244220526
45468CB00002B/1001